ALL THINGS ANIME AND MANGA

ANIME WORLD

HAL MARCOVITZ

ReferencePoint
Press®

San Diego, CA

About the Author

Hal Marcovitz is a former newspaper reporter and columnist. The author of more than two hundred books for young readers, he makes his home in Chalfont, Pennsylvania.

For more information, contact:
ReferencePoint Press, Inc.
PO Box 27779
San Diego, CA 92198
www.ReferencePointPress.com

LIBRARY OF CONGRESS CATALOGING-IN-PUBLICATION DATA

Names: Marcovitz, Hal, author.
Title: Anime world / by Hal Marcovitz.
Description: San Diego, CA : ReferencePoint Press, Inc., 2024. | Series:
   All things anime and manga | Includes bibliographical references and
   index.
Identifiers: LCCN 2023009460 (print) | LCCN 2023009461 (ebook) | ISBN
   9781678205164 (library binding) | ISBN 9781678205171 (ebook)
Subjects: LCSH: Animated films--Japan--Juvenile literature. | Animated
   television programs--Japan--Juvenile literature.
Classification: LCC NC1766.J3 M283 2024 (print) | LCC NC1766.J3 (ebook) |
   DDC 791.43/340952--dc23/eng/20230315
LC record available at https://lccn.loc.gov/2023009460
LC ebook record available at https://lccn.loc.gov/2023009461

CONTENTS

ANIME AT THE OLYMPICS

When the women's rhythmic gymnastics team from Uzbekistan took to the floor at the 2021 Summer Olympics in Tokyo, Japan, the fans cheered wildly. Their performances did not garner any medals, but the crowd did not care. They were expressing their delight at the team members competing in leotards that resembled the costume worn by the hugely popular anime character Sailor Moon. "Seeing them adopt a part of Japanese culture like this makes me so happy," a Japanese gymnastics fan told the publication *Otaku USA*, which covers anime culture. "I hope someone will tell them how grateful we are."[1]

Sailor Moon made her debut in comic books published in Japan in the early 1990s. She is a teen bestowed with magical powers; she and her team members, known as the Sailor Scouts, use these powers to save Earth from all manner of evildoers. Soon after making her debut in Japanese comic books, or manga, the character and her adventures were adapted into an animated, or anime, series produced for Japanese television. A few years later it was exported to many other countries, including the United States.

Nearly three decades after making her debut, Sailor Moon remains one of the most popular characters in anime. According to American anime critic Katie Gill, the series helped revolutionize the role of women not only in anime but in other forms of action-and-adventure entertainment as well:

> The magical girls in *Sailor Moon* faced problems that tended to be on a greater scale than something like a grumpy neighbor, a disagreement between friends, or performing at a big concert. They had to deal with those kinds of problems, sure . . . but they were also withstanding supernatural evil actively trying to kill them on a daily basis. *Sailor Moon* drew upon the action aspect of more traditional boys' shows as the Sailor Scouts regularly battled evil using their magic powers and, occasionally, their fists. Likewise, the stakes were much higher than in previous magical girl stories. While the specific motivations shifted, each final villain had essentially the same goal: take over the world. There was so much more on the line here, compared to the relatively mundane conflicts of the cute witches and magical pop idols that came before. [2]

TOUGHNESS AND ZEAL

Given the toughness and zeal associated with Sailor Moon, it should not have come as a surprise to see athletes adopt the spirit of her character at the Olympics. In fact, Sailor Moon is just one of hundreds of very popular anime characters in Japan, where television and cinema are dominated by the art form. Moreover, anime characters are often enlisted by Japanese manufacturers and retailers to appear in their advertisements, selling products to Japanese consumers. Anime characters are often featured in television commercials, on billboards and the sides of buses, and in print advertising as well.

The culture of anime is not limited to Japan. Along with automobiles, cameras,

> "The magical girls in *Sailor Moon* faced problems that tended to be on a greater scale than something like a grumpy neighbor, a disagreement between friends, or performing at a big concert."[2]
>
> —Anime critic Katie Gill

The women's rhythmic gymnastics team from Uzbekistan, wearing Sailor Moon–themed costumes, thrills fans at the 2021 Summer Olympics in Tokyo. Nearly three decades after making her debut, Sailor Moon remains one of the most popular characters in anime.

electronics and similar products, anime is among Japan's most popular exports. Between 2013 and 2022, the anime studio Toei Animation released four films in its enormously popular *Dragon Ball* series. The four films have collectively earned more than $289 million in worldwide box office revenue. The films feature the character Son Goku, a martial arts expert gifted with magical powers. "Films based on some of the most popular anime series can compete with major Hollywood films now," says Miki Niina, vice president of the Los Angeles–based film production company Eleven Arts, which specializes in bringing anime features to US audiences. "That didn't happen often a decade ago."[3]

IMPACTING INTERNATIONAL CULTURE

Back at the Tokyo Olympics, the women's rhythmic gymnastics competition was not the only place spectators could see the influence of anime. Prior to the start of the Olympics, organizers of the games announced that a dozen anime characters would be designated as "ambassadors" for the Summer Olympics. (Among those characters were Sailor Moon and Son Goku.) The characters appeared in advertisements and at promotional events for the games. Also, actors dressed as the characters entertained fans during breaks in events at the various stadiums, arenas, and other venues that hosted the competitions during the Olympics. And, of course, the millions of fans who followed the Olympics through television coverage saw these characters as well. Given the growth and popularity of anime over the past several decades, there is no question that anime's influence can now be found well beyond the television sets and cinemas in Japan.

CHAPTER ONE

THE EVOLUTION OF ANIME

The character known as Astro Boy, introduced in the United States in the 1960s, was not really a boy. Although he expressed human emotions such as kindness, love, humor, and anger, he was actually a robot. To defeat each episode's villain, Astro Boy was able to rely on the power of flight, which he accomplished by turning his feet into jet engines.

Astro Boy was a very popular comic book and anime series in Japan when an American television executive visiting the Japanese capital of Tokyo turned on the television set in his hotel room and saw one of the episodes. The executive believed the series could find an audience in America. He contacted the Japanese producer of the show, obtained a few episodes on film, and sent them to the NBC network in America. Television producers at NBC liked what they saw and purchased the series with the intention of showing it to American viewers. For American audiences, though, there had to be some changes. American actors were hired to provide voices for the characters. Moreover, other efforts to "Americanize" the series were made as well. If, for example, a scene showing the characters eating with chopsticks was part of the episode, that scene was edited out.

The American television executives believed there was a very real need to edit out the cultural references to Japan.

Astro Boy made its debut on American television in 1963—just eighteen years after the end of World War II. The United States had joined the war in 1941 after Japanese military aircraft staged a surprise attack on the US Navy base at Pearl Harbor, Hawaii. Over the next four years, more than one hundred thousand members of the US military lost their lives in the Pacific Theater, the region of the war that largely pitted American forces against the Japanese military. Another two hundred thousand Americans sustained battlefield wounds and injuries in the war in the Pacific. Therefore, the television executives feared that many Americans remained bitter toward the Japanese. Indeed, it was very likely that the young children of many World War II veterans—including those who fought in the Pacific—would be watching *Astro Boy* on the television sets in their parents' living rooms. Jim Dodd, an executive with NBC, admitted, "We don't

Astro Boy (at right), introduced to television viewers in the United States in the 1960s, was not actually a boy. He was a robot with feet that turned into jet engines, allowing him to fly after and defeat any villain who crossed his path.

plan to advertise the fact that the series is being animated in Japan. We're not going to deny it, if anybody asks, but we're not going to publicize it, either. First of all, there are probably some buyers at [television] stations out there who haven't gotten over the fact that Japan was our enemy in World War II."[4]

CLOWNS AND DOORMEN

As it turned out, the NBC executives had little reason to worry about a backlash against their decision to air *Astro Boy*. Audiences in the United States as well as other countries embraced the adventures of the robot boy, and soon American television networks were scrambling to obtain other anime series from producers in Japan. In fact, by the 1960s those American television executives were able to choose from a large number of anime shows that were being shown daily on Japanese television and in the nation's cinemas. Another early anime favorite in America was *Speed Racer*. Speed Racer (the name of the main character) was

Another early anime favorite in America was Speed Racer (pictured here), *about a young race car driver who roamed the world in his super speedy Mach 5. In his travels, he invariably met up with evil villains bent on world domination.*

KIMBA AND SIMBA

Along with *Astro Boy* and *Speed Racer*, one of the first anime television series exported to America was *Kimba the White Lion*, which made its US debut in 1965. The series told of the heroic efforts of a young lion cub, Kimba, to protect the animals of the forest and defeat the predators—both animal and human—who threaten their safety.

Anime historians believe Kimba's story inspired the 1994 animated film *The Lion King*, which was produced by the Walt Disney Company. (The film was also adapted into a successful Broadway musical and was remade in a new film version in 2019.) For starters, there is a similarity in names: the young cub at the center of *The Lion King* is named Simba. The entertainment newspaper *Hollywood Reporter* notes,

> In *The Lion King*, the main villain is an evil lion named Scar who has a black mane and a scar over his left eye. In *Kimba*, the main villain is an evil lion named Claw who has a black mane and a scar in place of his left eye. Claw's henchmen include two spotted hyenas. Scar's henchmen include three spotted hyenas. . . . There are even early pieces of concept art for *The Lion King* that depict Simba as a white lion.

Pete Keeley, "Big Little Lions: Disney's New 'Lion King' Dodges the 'Kimba' Similarity Issue," *Hollywood Reporter*, July 22, 2019. www.hollywoodreporter.com.

a young race car driver who roamed the world in his super speedy car, the Mach 5. As Speed traveled from race to race, he invariably met up with evil villains bent on world domination. *Speed Racer* debuted on American television in 1967. By then, anime had blossomed into a major industry in Japan.

Anime made its debut in Japan in 1917 when artist Oten Shimokawa created a five-minute animated cartoon. At the time, the concept of animated films was still rather new. The first animated film was produced in 1908 by French artist Émile Cohl, who created the film by rendering seven hundred drawings, each showing minor movements by the film's clownish characters. Each drawing was then photographed with black and white motion picture film, resulting in the creation of the animated movie, which he named *Fantasmagorie*. The film lasts just over a minute in length.

THE END OF BENSHI NARRATION

The technology that enables film audiences to hear dialogue spoken by actors did not arrive until 1927 with the release of the American movie *The Jazz Singer*. Until then, silent films often provided written explanations, inserted into the scenes, to advise the audiences of what the actors were saying to each other. In Japan, theaters relied on the *benshi*—professional narrators who were hired by theaters to interpret the action on the screen to audiences.

During this era, benshi narrators were often at odds with anime producers who believed the narrators were misrepresenting their messages to audiences. This disagreement was finally settled in 1923 when the Great Kanto Earthquake hit Japan, destroying much of the city of Tokyo, including its many theaters. Anime studios started showing their films in other cities where benshi narrators were far less common. According to anime historian Jonathan Clements, "The disaster of the earthquake served to distance the industry from the traditional leanings of the Tokyo theatrical and benshi interest groups. . . . The Kanto Earthquake marks a watershed in many histories of Japanese film, not only as a great tragedy, but also as a liberating influence that freed the surviving filmmakers from tradition." By the time Tokyo's theaters were rebuilt, benshi narrators were no longer needed because spoken dialogue was now available for anime and other films.

Jonathan Clements, *Anime: A History*. New York: Bloomsbury, 2022, p. 35.

By the time Shimokawa created his first film, artists in other countries were pursuing the craft of animation. The first American to create an animated feature was newspaper cartoonist Winsor McCay; in 1911, he produced a two-minute film titled *Little Nemo*, featuring one of the characters from his cartoons. Similar to how Cohl produced his film, McCay rendered individual drawings—in the case of *Little Nemo*, some four thousand drawings—each showing a minor degree of movement, then photographed each drawing to make the black-and-white film.

Shimokawa took a much different route toward creating the first animated film in Japan. Instead of rendering and then photographing individual drawings, Shimokawa inked the images right onto the movie film itself. This was an intricate and undoubtedly painstaking process, but in the end he was able to produce a five-minute animated film titled *The Story of the Concierge Mukuzo Imokawa*, telling the humorous tale of a hotel doorman. (Anime historians believe *Concierge Mukuzo* was actually Shimokawa's third film, but it was the first to be shown in theaters. No records exist for his first two efforts.)

CEL ANIMATION

Following the premiere of *Concierge Mukuzo* in a Tokyo theater, other Japanese artists devoted their efforts to the new art form, and soon theaters across Japan were featuring anime films. By the 1920s and 1930s, several film studios had been established in Japan specifically to produce anime. Over the years such features as color film and sound were added to the productions.

In 1935 a Japanese studio established by animator Kenzo Masaoka released the film *Dance of the Teakettles*. Until then, Japanese artists had been creating films much the same way as Cohl and McCay by rendering thousands of individual drawings on paper, then photographing them. But Masaoka is believed to be the first Japanese animator to employ the use of "cel" animation. In cel animation, the drawings are made on transparent plastic sheets known as celluloid, or cels, then photographed using movie film. Using cels rather than ordinary paper to create the images provides a crisper, more detailed image. "Masaoka's innovations in sound and pictures made him a key figure in the development of Japanese animation," notes anime historian Jonathan Clements. He explains that Masaoka "played a vital role in transforming the industry from one in which a simply moving picture was regarded as noteworthy, to one in which animation was truly established as an art and craft."[5]

But the advancements in the art being made by Masaoka's studio and other Japanese animators would soon come to a halt. By the late 1930s, Japan had made many enemies across Asia, Europe, and North America, and war seemed inevitable. In 1941, Japanese military planes attacked Pearl Harbor. Japan soon joined Germany

> "[Kenzo] Masaoka's innovations in sound and pictures made him a key figure in the development of Japanese animation."[5]
>
> —Anime historian Jonathan Clements

and Italy as the Axis Powers—the enemies of America and the other Allied Powers.

ANIME AS PROPAGANDA

Still, even though Japan's government, military, and citizens were focused on battling the Allies, the anime industry in Japan remained busy. Military leaders were well aware of the popularity of anime among Japanese citizens and helped finance the production of numerous anime films that were screened for audiences at home as Japanese soldiers faced battle in the Pacific Theater.

However, the films were clearly produced as a form of propaganda—meaning the animators were under orders to produce films showing Japan bravely standing up to its enemies.

For example, the 1943 military-financed anime feature titled *Momotaro's Sea Eagle* depicts a Japanese attack on an Allied naval base known as Demon Island. The main character, the young and brave lad Momotaro, leads his plucky animal friends in the attack. Clearly, Demon Island resembled Pearl Harbor. Later, Americans who viewed the film noticed a familiar character: Bluto, the buffoonish villain found in the American comic strip and animated cartoon series *Popeye the Sailor*.

In the film, Bluto finds himself humiliated and defeated by Momotaro and the other heroic Japanese defenders. As Susan Napier, a professor of Japanese studies at Tufts University in Medford, Massachusetts, explains,

> The demons are represented as beefy Americans with horns on their heads, including an obvious homage to the character Bluto in the Popeye comic strips who, in rather un-demonic fashion, cries and blubbers as the navy ships explode around him. . . . In the original story, Momotaro's

"The demons are represented as beefy Americans with horns on their heads, including an obvious homage to the character Bluto in the Popeye comic strips."[6]

—Japanese studies professor Susan Napier

followers in the film are fewer and weaker than the well-equipped demons, but they nevertheless triumph over the larger, technologically advanced enemy.[6]

ANIMATED BUTTERFLIES

Momotaro and his friends may have been triumphing over their enemies on the screens in Japanese cinemas, but across the Pacific Theater, the war was hardly going in Japan's favor. Finally, in September 1945—less than a month after the United States had dropped atomic bombs on Hiroshima and Nagasaki—Japan surrendered. (By then, Germany and Italy had already been defeated by the Allies.) Japan's cities lay in ruins. The nation's economy—which had focused for years on little more than manufacturing weapons of war—was shattered.

Following Japan's surrender, America, Great Britain, and other Allies dispatched military leaders, diplomats, engineers, economists, and other professionals to Japan to help the nation establish

The United States dropped atomic bombs on Nagasaki (pictured) and Hiroshima—ending World War II. Western efforts to rebuild Japan's economy did not include reestablishing the anime industry; however, artists who survived the war set out to do just that.

a democratic government and rebuild its economy. Japan soon became an important member of the world economy, manufacturing and exporting automobiles, cameras, electronic devices, and many other products to the United States and other Western nations. But these foreign experts had little interest or expertise in reestablishing the Japanese anime industry.

Moreover, the peace treaty the Allies signed with Japan not only enabled the Japanese to export goods to the West but also enabled the United States and other Western nations to send their products to Japan. Among the American-made products that soon found their way to Japan were animated features produced by Hollywood studios. Soon after Japan's surrender to the Allies, Japanese animators found themselves facing competition from Western animators.

In the years leading up to the war, the Japanese government refused to permit such American animation studios as the Walt Disney Company to export its films to Japan. That changed after the war. Japanese moviegoers were able to see films such as *Snow White and the Seven Dwarfs* and *Pinocchio* in theaters in Tokyo and other cities. And those Japanese audiences, eager for light and enjoyable entertainment that would help them put the war years behind them, flocked to the theaters to see those American-made animated features. This put Japanese animators in the difficult position of not only trying to rebuild their once-thriving industry but also facing competition from foreign animators who were now exporting their films to Japan.

Still, Japanese artists who survived the war persevered in reestablishing the nation's anime studios. Indeed, in November 1945—about two months after Japan formally surrendered—Kenzo Masaoka founded the Shin Nihon Dogasha studio in the city of Kyoto. In 1946, the studio produced its first film: *Cherry Blossoms: Spring Fantasy*. The film told no story. It simply followed a pair of animated butterflies as they fluttered through a picturesque background of gardens, people, and animals.

The film was never shown in theaters; rather, Masaoka screened the film for small groups of Japanese artists, hoping to interest them in becoming animators. The tactic worked, and soon Masaoka's studio was busy producing animated films for Japanese audiences. Other studios were established in Japan as well. Anime historians report that by the 1950s, these studios employed some five hundred artists to produce features for Japanese audiences.

AN INDUSTRY WORTH BILLIONS

Of course, few people outside of Japan were aware of the rebirth and growth of anime—that is, until 1963, when that American television network executive visiting Japan turned on the television set in his hotel room and discovered an episode of *Astro Boy*. Today, the animation industry in Japan is enormous, producing films not only for Japanese audiences but foreign audiences as well. According to the New York City–based market research firm Statista, the animation industry in Japan earns more than $19 billion a year. Moreover, Statista reports that some 150 separate studios in Japan produce more than two hundred animated features each year, providing content for television series, films, and video games. Gaku Narita, a Disney executive charged with developing anime features for the well-known American entertainment corporation, comments, "We're seeing more and more appetite for anime throughout all demographics, in all countries. It's increasingly becoming a borderless form of mass entertainment."[7]

Now, more than a century after Oten Shimokawa inked those first images onto movie film, Japan's animation studios have carved out a significant niche in the international entertainment industry. Anime survived a world war and, thanks largely to a robot boy, found an international audience that enthusiastically welcomes the adventures of the many characters who emerge from the imaginations of Japan's huge community of animators.

CHAPTER TWO

THE STORIES TOLD THROUGH ANIME

Yuri Katsuki is a twenty-three-year-old figure skater who finds his career in a downward spiral. After finishing in last place in an important international event, Yuri returns home to Japan. He is despondent and questions whether he will ever achieve success and fame in his chosen sport. Still, while clearly depressed, Yuri returns to the ice rink to practice his routine. Unknown to Yuri, a friend records the practice session and uploads the video to an internet platform. Victor Nikiforov, a noted Russian figure skating coach, sees the video and believes Yuri has the talent to become a world champion. Victor travels to Japan, takes Yuri under his wing, and trains him for his future competitions.

Of course, throughout the ensuing story there are many dramas ahead. Yuri tangles with rivals—most notably, JJ, another figure skater. Yuri continues to question his own abilities and motivations, but Victor stands behind him, and slowly Yuri gains confidence.

Yuri is the star of an anime series titled *Yuri!!! on Ice*, which debuted on Japanese television in 2016 and has since been made available to audiences in other countries. Author and anime critic Melissa See admits,

I wasn't expecting to fall in love with *Yuri!!! on Ice*. At first glance, I thought it was going to be a "typical sports anime" with one-dimensional characters and repetitive episodes that rely almost entirely on the sport of choice to carry it, in lieu of an actual plot.

My perception changed immediately within the first few minutes of the show, when Yuri locks himself in a bathroom stall to call his mother and shortly thereafter starts crying because he came in last place during his competition, firmly believing that he failed. This is our protagonist. He's not confident. He's not strong. Instead, he's hiding from both his loss and those around him.[8]

Moreover, fans of *Yuri!!! on Ice* do not see any superheroes at the center of the figure skater's story. Sailor Moon and the Sailor Scouts are never called on to swoop in to save Yuri—as well as

Yuri!!! on Ice is not a typical sports anime despite its taking place in the world of figure skating. This imaginary world nonetheless reflects the real world of Japanese figure skating (Japanese skating champion Yuzuru Hanyu is pictured).

the rest of the world—from an evil predator. Astro Boy, Speed Racer, and Son Goku are nowhere to be found either.

Although superheroes provided the early foundation for anime—and they certainly remain a staple of the art form today—Japanese animation has long since moved beyond the realm of superheroes to include dramatic stories, romances, comedies, mysteries, and other genres found throughout the wider world of entertainment. In fact, the desire by Japanese animators to tell stories more typical of ordinary life in contemporary culture dates back to the 1930s. The first anime "talkie"—meaning the characters spoke in dialogue that could be heard by the audience—was the film *The World of Power and Women*. The film, which was released in Japanese theaters in 1933, was hardly intended for a young audience. Instead, the film told the story of a husband whose wife learns, from talking in his sleep, that he is having an extramarital affair.

REFLECTING JAPANESE CULTURE

The World of Power and Women may have been aimed at a more adult audience, but soon Japanese animators with an interest in producing such stories found their resources rather limited. World War II soon intervened, and anime turned more toward propaganda. Then, following the war, animators found their biggest fans in young audiences—meaning more opportunities for superheroes. But attitudes started changing in the 1970s with such shows as *Tomorrow's Joe*, a dramatic series about a young juvenile delinquent who turns to the sport of boxing to rebuild his life; and *Lupin the Third*, about a dapper, well-spoken gentleman thief who travels the world looking for valuable treasures to steal. (Both series have spawned many sequels and reboots and remain popular well into the twenty-first century.)

According to Patrick Drazen, an American anime historian, the genres of comedy, drama, mystery, romance, and tragedy have found their way into anime because the art form truly reflects Japanese culture:

Remember that Japanese culture goes back about 3,000 years. Religious mythology, regional folktales, histories from one or both sides of various conflicts, modern "urban legends"; these and more feed into a pop culture and get reflected back, and it's surprising how echoes of the past keep popping up in Japan's anime present. . . . Finding these stories, and more, salted [throughout] Japanese cartoons made me realize that these media were anything but childish and trivial, as comic books and cartoons in the West have the reputation for being.[9]

ROMANCE AND COMEDIES

And so, stories about troubled young people, dapper criminals, and even tales focused squarely on romance are found throughout the world of anime. By 2023, one of the most popular anime romantic series was *Tomo-chan Is a Girl!* The series tells the story of a teenage girl, Tomo Aizawa, who develops a crush on

The manga series Lupin the Third *spawned hundreds of anime episodes. The storyline—which revolves around a gentleman thief who travels the world looking for valuable treasures to steal—reflected a change in attitudes and audience interests.*

a boy named Jun Kubota. At first, though, Jun regards Tomo as no more than a friend. While the two were classmates in middle school, he did not even know Tomo was a girl because she wore her hair cut short and never dressed in skirts. Tomo soon realizes that she has been living her life as a tomboy, and so she sets out to feminize herself—making herself more alluring to Jun. The series covers her obstacles, errors, and successes as she searches for love. But the series also delves into Jun's life as he slowly realizes he is attracted to Tomo and ponders whether he wants her more as a friend or as a romantic partner. Chicago-based journalist and anime critic Isaiah Colbert writes,

> While this comedy of errors provides a good balance to the two's slow-burn romance, the show never lets its jokes overshadow the pain Tomo feels when she tries to act more girly to impress Jun. Tomo doesn't suffer alone, either. Jun gets flustered whenever he notices that Tomo is a lovestruck girl who's dying to have her feelings reciprocated. Tomo and Jun's love story is something I've been dying to experience from modern romantic comedies: a simple yet relatable romantic storyline where its characters aren't caricatures.[10]

The story of Tomo and Jun is light and heartwarming, and it does have its moments of comedy. Another series that features a touch of comedy is a 2016 anime movie titled *Your Name*. The film opens with a teenage boy named Taki going to bed one night in his Tokyo home. When he wakes up the next morning, Taki has discovered he has turned into a girl named Mitsuha. Miles away, in the Japanese countryside, Mitsuha wakes up in her own bed and discovers she has turned into a boy named Taki. In other words, overnight the two teens have swapped bodies. Luckily for Mitsuha

STAN LEE'S FAILED ATTEMPT AT ANIME

Stan Lee is best known as a cofounder of Marvel Comics and the creator of such characters as Spider-Man, Iron Man, and the Incredible Hulk. These characters eventually made their way from comic books to television and film adaptations, both as animated and live-action characters.

Lee also partnered with a Japanese production company, Studio Bones, to create the anime series *Heroman*. The series focuses on Joey, a young orphan who is bullied at school. One day he meets a powerful robot, Heroman. The two form an alliance, with Joey taking over the controls of the robot and providing Heroman with the guidance to take on criminals and other evildoers.

Heroman ran for twenty-six episodes on Japanese television in 2010 but was not renewed for a second season. And despite Lee's tremendous influence over animation in the United States, the series was never televised in America. Critics found the stories lacked originality. One critic wrote on the website THEM Anime Reviews, "Heroman, despite being the titular character is nothing more than a toy that was given super powers and with no personality of his own; sure he's a cool looking hulk of a superhero, but aside from a boyhood fantasy come to life, what is there?"

THEM Anime Reviews, "Heroman," 2015. www.themanime.org.

and Taki, the body swaps are only temporary. Soon, they find their own bodies returned to them and life proceeds normally—until it happens again and again and again. There are many comedic moments as the two characters bounce back and forth between genders, stumbling to learn that boys and girls have different attitudes, feelings, and emotions.

The comedy is real but so is the romance. Anime critic Chris Stuckmann notes,

> While at first, Taki and Mitsuha are both urgently searching for ways to end this star-crossed exchange, soon enough, they begin to look forward to the time spent as the other person. They become invested in each other's life and their concerns. Before long, their own lives become placeholders for the days they wake up as the opposite person. In this way, a beautiful bond is formed between the two, leading to significantly intimate discoveries for both of them.[11]

The anime movie Your Name features a touch of both comedy and romance. Its central characters are two teens, a boy and a girl who have never met, who suddenly find they have swapped bodies.

Although both characters grow into adulthood apart from one another, they meet years later in an unexpected and chance encounter and fall in love.

DARK AND MYSTERIOUS

Audiences may have been delighted to follow the stories of Taki and Mitsuha as well as Tomo and Jun, but anime creators often pursue much darker stories. Indeed, one of the darkest anime series premiered on Japanese television in 2008, spawning additional seasons as well as sequels. Titled *Black Butler*, the series features a twelve-year-old central character, Ciel Phantomhive, who lives in London during the 1880s.

As the plot unfolds, viewers learn Ciel's parents have been murdered. The boy is kidnapped by the killers and sold into slavery, where he is physically abused by his captors, who are members of a sadistic cult. To escape from his captors, Ciel forges a pact with a demon named Sebastian—the Black Butler—to seek revenge on Ciel's tormentors and avenge the deaths of his parents. And while pursuing the boy's enemies, Ciel and Sebastian find themselves solving other vicious crimes in nineteenth-century London.

The series draws on supernatural elements, but it is not light fare and is not intended for young audiences. According to anime critic Via Erhard,

> *Black Butler* is one of the best gothic anime series for adult viewers who love darkly sophisticated humor and anime stories that don't shy away from some of the most taboo subjects. This stunningly designed anime has a beautiful art style and some of the most terrifying and courageous characters of all time. This anime is shocking, violent, and even gory at times, but it's also one of the most thought-provoking ones with meaningful stories and great character arcs.[12]

RETURN OF THE SUPERHEROES

Characters such as Ciel and Sebastian may help solve crimes and bring the killers of Ciel's parents to justice, but they are hardly examples of righteous and heroic anime characters. Anime zoomed into intense popularity thanks to such characters as Astro Boy, Speed Racer, and Sailor Moon—real do-gooders whose only intentions were to protect the vulnerable and save Earth from evil predators. Certainly, those roots remain in place today. In the

ANIME SOAP OPERAS

Soap operas became a staple of American television in the 1950s. Invariably aired during weekday afternoons and aimed at audiences primarily composed of housewives, the soap operas, today often referred to simply as "soaps," feature melodramatic themes of romance but also backstabbing, adultery, and jealousy. The genre earned the name *soap operas* because in the early days they were usually sponsored by laundry detergent manufacturers.

Soap opera–style entertainment has also found a home in anime. Among the most popular of the anime soap operas are *School Days*, featuring a love triangle among the characters Makoto, Sekai, and Kotonoha; and *Given*, which follows the often-rocky love affairs involving two members of a rock band. Another popular anime soap is *Rumbling Hearts*, which follows the love affair of Takayuki and Haruka and what happens after Haruka wakes up from a coma and discovers Takayuki has a new girlfriend—Haruka's best friend, Mitsuki. And finally, anime soap opera fans can follow *Scum's Wish*, in which both main characters, Hanabi and Mugi, carry on a love affair—but unknown to the two lovers, they are cheating on each other.

contemporary world of anime, superheroes continue to dominate the genre.

Dozens of television series and cinematic films featuring anime superheroes are released by Japanese animation studios each year. Over the years, one of the most popular anime superhero stories has been *Cyborg 009*. It tells the tale of teenager Joe Shimamura, who wakes up one day in a laboratory where he discovers that evil scientists intend to turn him into a robot. Joe escapes, but he retains some of the robotic components inserted into his body, which give him superpowers. He soon teams up with eight other teens who have similarly been transformed into "cyborgs"—half-human, half-robot beings—to fight a terrorist network known as Black Ghost, which seeks to spark worldwide warfare.

Another popular anime series focusing on superheroes is *Jujutsu Kaisen*, first released in 2020, that tells the story of an evil entity known as Cursed Energy which dispatches evil beings known as Curses to terrorize Earth. The protagonist is Yuta Itadori, a high school student who uses his superior martial arts skills to fight back against the Curses.

Not all anime superheroes are male characters. In 2002, a female superhero story, *Tokyo Mew Mew*, made its debut as a Japanese television series. (The series was rebooted in 2022 with the title *Tokyo Mew Mew New*.) The series tells the story of a teenage girl, Ichigo Momomiya, who is struck by a mysterious ray that gives her superhuman powers that provide her with the skills of an endangered species of cat. She soon meets four other girls with similar powers drawn from endangered species. They pledge to form a team—Tokyo Mew Mew—to protect Earth against extraterrestrial criminals who threaten the planet. Anime critic Alexander Case explains,

> As part of all of this, Ichigo is also trying to juggle a school life with her Magical Girl life, including a burgeoning romance with the school prince, Masaya Aoyama, who is the star of the [martial arts] club and a passionate conservationist. This leads to a side plot with the two coming to terms with their feelings for each other, while Ichigo tries to preserve her secret identity, with varying degrees of success. . . . It's definitely a show that is dependent on the writing and chemistry of the characters to do the heavy lifting.[13]

Fans of anime can find hundreds of similar stories, most of which are essentially pitting characters possessing superhuman abilities against villains with evil intentions. Sometimes these superheroes are troubled, but they nevertheless overcome self-doubt and depression to rise to their nobler cause: to save Earth from villainy. Of course, if anime fans do grow weary of such stories, they can always fall back on the dramas, comedies, and romances that continually emerge from the sketch pads of Japan's anime producers.

"[*Tokyo Mew Mew* is] definitely a show that is dependent on the writing and chemistry of the characters to do the heavy lifting."[13]

—Anime critic Alexander Case

CHAPTER THREE

THE UNIQUE STYLE OF ANIME ART

Look at the faces of those around you, and it is likely you will see various (yet subtle) sizes and shapes of people's eyes. Among these shapes are almond eyes, in which the opposite ends of each eye taper, forming the shape of an almond; down-turned eyes, in which the taper of each eye tends to point toward the tops of the cheeks below; and close-set eyes, in which the space between the right and left eye is relatively narrow, owing, mostly, to a person's tinier-than-average nose.

Now look at the face of the typical anime character, and you will find none of these attributes are true. Virtually all characters in anime have enormous round eyes, clearly dominating their faces. This trend was started after World War II, when the anime industry of Japan was rebuilding itself after years of armed conflict. As anime artists got back to work, they found the supplies they needed to produce their films were in short supply—particularly the transparent cels they needed to create their images.

One of the pioneering anime artists of the postwar era was Osamu Tezuka. Because of the cel shortage, Tezuka realized he would need to tell his stories with as few cels as possible. Tezuka found that he could move the stories along faster by relying more on the facial expressions of his characters than on their physical movements across the screen. Those physical movements would have required more cels than Tezuka's studio had available. Tezuka concluded that the easiest way to display emotion in his characters was through their eyes. And so, Tezuka made his characters' eyes big and round so that he could more easily show happiness, sadness, fear, anger, and other emotions. As Japanese studies professor Susan Napier explains,

"Compared to American animation, Japanese cartoons were more cheaply produced, involving fewer cels. This led to a different style of animation, less fluid and nuanced."[14]

—Japanese studies professor Susan Napier

Compared to American animation, Japanese cartoons were more cheaply produced, involving fewer cels. This led to a different style of animation, less fluid and nuanced. . . . With less ability to do subtle facial expressions, animation artists concentrated on the eyes, leading to the distinctive "anime" look of many characters who expressed their feelings through their large liquid eyes.[14]

Tezuka's influence on the faces of virtually all characters in anime has endured. Regardless of whether the character is an innocent young child or the cruelest supernatural demon, their eyes will almost always be big, round, and expressive.

MANGA AND THE ROOTS OF ANIME ART

As the shape of the characters' eyes illustrates, anime has a definitive artistic style that sets it apart from most animated series and films produced in America and other nations. And that style has its roots in manga. Many anime characters are born on the pages of manga, itself a huge industry in Japan. According to the San Francisco–based market research firm Grand View Research, in 2021 manga publishers earned roughly $19 billion by producing thousands of titles a year. (The word *manga* stems from a Japanese term for "whimsical pictures.")

In Japan, manga serves as an important testing ground for animated television series and films. If a manga series proves

Large, round, expressive eyes are the most noticeable physical feature in most anime characters. Early Japanese animators focused on the eyes because they lacked the materials to portray fluid movements and subtle expressions.

popular among Japanese readers, chances are the stories and characters will be adapted into anime. That model for creating new animated films and series is certainly true in America and other countries as well. Superman, Batman, Wonder Woman, Spider-Man, and many other popular characters in American animation—and live-action films as well—got their starts on the pages of comic books.

But there is a significant difference between how Superman and other characters are rendered on the screen for American animated features and how Japanese characters are drawn for anime. In animated films featuring Superman and Spider-Man, the heroes can often be seen swooping through the sky, performing all manner of acrobatic maneuvers to catch the villains or save imperiled victims from disaster. But in anime, the characters largely mimic the very static poses and postures that can be found in their manga editions. In other words, there is far less action and movement in anime than is found in Western-style animation. As Christopher Hart, an American artist and author who teaches the techniques of manga and anime, notes,

> Western-style animation expresses itself primarily through movement. The more a character moves, the "better" the animation is thought to be. So, it's not surprising that animation producers in the West typically redesign comic book characters for television, simplifying them to allow for greater movement. Although anime characters are also licensed from comic books, emphasis is placed on retaining the integrity of the original comic. The detail and subtlety in the drawings are not sacrificed to allow for greater movement. As a result, anime has the appearance of a real comic book come to life.[15]

Moreover, according to Hart, even decades after the rebirth of anime following World War II, anime production companies remain notoriously frugal when it comes to investing in the actual art shown on the screen. Therefore, today's anime artists must find ways to emphasize the action on the screen without actually inserting much action into the scene. And, as Tezuka found he could do years ago, today's anime artists accomplish that task largely through the facial expressions on their characters. Hart explains, "Japanese budgets for anime are usually less, per episode, than western animation budgets. Anime makes up for that with greater emphasis on character design, pacing, and intensity, creating scenes that appear to burst with action while the action is rather limited."[16]

KAWAII CULTURE

Of course, there is more to the typical anime character than his or her facial expressions. After all, each character has arms, legs, torsos, and other body parts as well as hairstyles and costumes.

THE TINIEST DETAILS

According to author and animation teacher Christopher Hart, when designing characters that appear in anime, the tiniest details help define the personalities of those characters. For example, does a female character wear glasses? If she does, Hart advises, "Girls who wear glasses are never dorky. In fact, they're cool and stylish. Glasses are an accessory, like jewelry. They make a statement. . . . Don't skimp on the size of the lenses. Make them too small and you'll give those gorgeous . . . eyes a claustrophobic look."

Schoolboys have their own unique looks as well. "Schoolboys share common characteristics," says Hart. "They have an affable and bright-eyed appearance. The physique has yet to fill out. (Usually, only the upper classmen are tall.) He's still awkward, the clothes are a little unkempt—for example, shirt out, sleeves rolled up, tie loosened, and so on. Keep these general parameters in mind when thinking up your own schoolboy characters."

Christopher Hart, *Mangamania Girl Power! Drawing Fabulous Females for Japanese Comics*. New York: Sixth & Spring, 2009, p. 18.

Christopher Hart, *The Master Guide to Drawing Anime: How to Draw Original Characters from Simple Templates*. New York: Sixth & Spring, 2015, p. 47.

And again, anime has distinctive styles for all of these elements of its characters. In many anime productions, the heroes and other characters in each story are designed to reflect Japan's culture of *kawaii*—the nation's unabashed love for all things cute. Anybody who has ever traveled to Japan has undoubtedly noticed the preponderance of the Hello Kitty images throughout the nation's cities. Hello Kitty is a puffy kitten of unbridled cuteness, adorning advertisements, clothing, smartphone cases, and many other consumer products manufactured in Japan. In short, Hello Kitty is a predominant symbol of kawaii culture.

Hello Kitty did not start showing up around Japan until the 1970s. However, historians trace kawaii culture back to the early 1900s, when a Tokyo stationery store started featuring cute characters on its envelopes, paper, and other products, hoping to sell them to young girls. Unexpectedly, adult customers were drawn to the characters as well. By the time the first manga and anime artists were designing their characters, kawaii culture was very much a part of Japanese life.

And so, when anime artists design their characters, they often try to add a kawaii look to their physical qualities. For example, large, round eyes can be cute but so can hairstyles, particularly for female characters. "Hair is a very important feature," says Hart. "It's used to add glamour, to add size to the head (and thereby increase the visual presence of the character) and to carve out a unique identity for a character whose face might otherwise look similar to others. In fact, when magical girls are members of teams, they often look so similar that their hairstyles are one of the primary ways to tell them apart."[17] Therefore, Hart says, avid viewers of anime will notice that female characters rarely wear the same hairstyles; characters wearing ponytails, long wavy hair, ringlets, curls, and buns are all likely to be found in the same scenes. Moreover, their hair colors are likely to be vivid: bright oranges, blacks, yellows, reds, and even greens and blues. And it is also likely that no two female characters sharing an anime screen will have the same color hair either.

Kawaii culture can be found in characters' costumes as well. Sailor Moon and her Sailor Scouts are brave and magical fighters,

Hello Kitty, the puffy kitten of unbridled cuteness, is the essence of kawaii culture. Hello Kitty can be found on advertisements, clothing, smartphone cases, and many other consumer products manufactured in Japan.

often called on to save the planet from interstellar villains. They do so while dressed in short skirts, knee-high boots or high heels, and white blouses adorned with colorful bows. These garments are known as the *senshi* ("warrior") uniforms of the Sailor Scouts. In other words, the Sailor Scouts go to war to save life on Earth while still looking very kawaii.

THE SHONEN UNIVERSE

Women and girls are not the only anime characters designed with kawaii culture in mind; men and boys also must project a level of cuteness. "You see this super popular character everywhere," notes Hart. "He's intense and never gives up, no matter how much danger stands in his way. Oh sure, he takes his share of hits, but he's resilient and keeps coming back. Clean-cut, nice looking, and trustworthy, you wouldn't mind if he dated your sister."[18] Thin, athletic, muscled, usually smiling with perfect teeth and with hair that is largely free flowing and uncombed, the male anime hero certainly falls into kawaii culture in his appeal to female fans.

Nonetheless, he is meant to appeal to male fans as well—while still retaining the kawaii quality so important to Japanese audiences. In fact, male characters often fall into a category of anime known as *shonen*—a genre aimed at younger teenage boys. The *Dragon Ball* films and television series are regarded as part of the shonen universe. The main character, Son Goku, is muscled and tough when he needs to be, but he also has black hair that is comically spikey, and he invariably wears a puckish expression. Likewise, his large, round eyes are often rendered to give him a screwball, cross-eyed look.

And, very often, even the villains project a level of kawaii culture. They might be smug evildoers, but anime artists often draw them as supercool and matinee-idol handsome. "Cool, charming, dangerous," agrees Hart. "Maybe he's a part of a gang. Maybe he's an enemy of a gang. Either way, he loves danger."[19]

> "You see this super popular character everywhere. He's intense and never gives up, no matter how much danger stands in his way."[18]
>
> —Artist and author Christopher Hart

The Dragon Ball *films and television series are part of the shonen universe. The main character, Son Goku (pictured), is muscled and tough, but he also has comically spikey black hair and a screwball, cross-eyed look.*

ANIME'S INFLUENCE OUTSIDE JAPAN

As anime has become more and more popular in America and other Western nations, animation studios have taken notice of the artistic styles of anime—the big, expressive eyes of the characters and the reflection of kawaii culture. And that is why more and more television series and films produced by American studios have adopted many of the artistic techniques that fans have long found in anime. For example, the American animated series *Teen Titans,* which can be found on the Cartoon Network, leaves an anime impression on its viewers. The main characters are teenage superheroes whose stories have been published over the years by the American comic book company DC Comics. Among the main characters are Robin, the teenage companion of Batman; Raven, a teenage girl with supernatural powers; Cyborg, a troubled, superintelligent teen with robotic limbs; and Beast Boy, a young hero who can change into the animal of his choice.

Many fans of *Teen Titans* undoubtedly notice the anime influence in how the characters have been rendered by the show's artists. That is largely because the American producers of the show

WHERE TO STUDY ANIME

To learn the skills of an anime artist, students would do well to enroll in universities in Japan. Kyoto Seika University is regarded as one of the nation's top anime schools. But to enroll in Kyoto Seika or another art school in Japan, foreign students would, of course, need to first learn the Japanese language.

College-level art schools in the United States offer courses in animation, but these courses do not focus on the specific techniques of anime. Still, at many art schools, students with an interest in anime have taken it upon themselves to develop their talents. For example, the noted art school the Pratt Institute in New York City features the student-run Anime & Manga Club. One of the club's missions is to provide students with training in the techniques of anime. According to the institute, "The Anime & Manga Club aims to promote and provide a space for the discussion, creation, learning and enjoyment of anime, comics, games, and Japanese culture/entertainment media."

Pratt Institute, "Anime & Manga Club," 2023. https://pratt.campuslabs.com.

hired an animation studio in Japan to illustrate the series. Viewers of *Teen Titans* have certainly noticed the large eyes and often comical facial expressions of the characters as well as their unruly hairstyles—all standard techniques found in anime. Anime critic Jordan C. Stewart comments that "spikey hair is a common hairstyle seen on protagonists in shonen anime and manga—that is media aimed at young boys and [tending] to be action-based—so it makes sense that an action-driven show like *Teen Titans* would choose that style for some of their characters."[20]

> "Spikey hair is a common hairstyle seen on protagonists in shonen anime and manga—that is media aimed at young boys and [tending] to be action-based."[20]
>
> —Anime critic Jordan C. Stewart

Anime has a definite artistic style that makes it immediately recognizable to fans: big eyes, emotive facial expressions, spikey hair, and colorful costumes worn by the main characters. Given the rise in popularity in the United States and elsewhere, it should not come as a surprise when fans of *Teen Titans* and other series and films come to realize that, more and more, their favorite shows are reflecting the influence of anime.

CHAPTER FOUR

THE CULTURE OF ANIME

Fans of pop singer Ariana Grande could not help but notice that she had a new tattoo on her right wrist in 2018. The tattoo depicts ten-year-old Chihiro Ogino, a character in the 2001 anime film *Spirited Away*. The film tells the story of Chihiro's struggle to free herself and her parents from a cult of witches and evil spirits who have enslaved her and turned her mother and father into pigs.

The film was enormously successful not only in Japan but in the United States and other countries as well, earning $355 million at the worldwide box office. Moreover, *Spirited Away*, written and directed by renowned animator Hayao Miyazaki, won the 2003 Academy Award for best animated feature.

Grande says she decided to get the tattoo of Chihiro out of admiration for the character and what she represents:

Chihiro's growth into a capable individual is a core factor to the movement of *Spirited Away*'s plot. During her adventure in the Spirit World, she matures from an easily-scared girl with a child-like personality to match her age to a hard-working, responsible, and brave young girl who has learned to put her fears aside for those she cares for. To protect her friends and rescue her parents from a spell that has turned them into livestock, Chihiro sheds her former personality and adapts to her environment to become a courageous, quick-witted and reliable girl.[21]

Tattooed on the wrist of pop singer Ariana Grande is an image of ten-year-old Chihiro Ogino (pictured center), a character in the acclaimed 2001 anime film Spirited Away. *Fans worldwide have found many ways to show their devotion to anime.*

The decision by one of the world's most popular entertainers to get a tattoo depicting an anime character illustrates how anime has developed a worldwide following of fans who are willing to show their devotion to anime in very public ways. Not only do fans line up at theaters to see new releases and stream anime films and series at home, but each year tens of thousands of fans also attend conventions in many major cities. Looking for an anime group to join on social media? There are hundreds available on numerous social media platforms.

Grande is not the only famous entertainer who has embraced anime. The rap star Megan Thee Stallion often wears costumes on stage resembling those worn by her favorite anime characters, and she has told interviewers that she watches anime every day. "I literally begin my day watching anime, and I end my day watching anime,"[22] says the singer. Among her favorite series are *Hunter x Hunter*, which tells the story of a young boy who aspires to become a member of "The Hunters," a secret society of heroes who are called on to perform daredevil missions; and *Attack on Titan*, which follows a young hero's journey to defend his city against evil giants. Unlike Grande, Megan has not acquired a tattoo of an anime character, but she often employs nail artists to paint images of her favorite anime characters onto her very long fingernails.

ANIME CONVENTIONS

In getting her tattoo of Chihiro, Grande was not unlike many fans of anime. Tattoo artists in America and other countries report that anime characters are very much in demand by their clients. A Colorado-based tattoo artist known as Tashy says she has long been a fan of anime herself and is always delighted when a client requests a tattoo to reflect his or her love for the art form. She explains,

> I've always loved the art style of anime and other cartoons from when I was a kid and now as an adult. . . . I think anime is so beautiful and love that my clients feel the same way. I also love the fact that someone can love an anime show so much that they want to get it permanently on their body. To me it shows that something that can seem "silly" or "imma-ture" to some people can mean something much more to other people, like the people who get my tattoos.[23]

In fact, anime has become such a large part of the tattoo world that twice each year tattoo artists and their fans meet at the Anime Ink Conventions. At the conventions, fans can book sessions with the nation's top anime tattoo artists, shop for other anime-related art, such as large prints featuring anime characters, and enter cosplay contests where the anime-themed costumes they wear are judged and awarded prizes.

If fans have no interest in getting themselves tattooed, there is no shortage of conventions each year that enable them to simply join other fans in sharing their interests in anime. According to the organization AnimeCons, which organizes anime conventions, there are anime conventions scheduled for virtually every weekend in the year among many American and European cities. In fact, in 2023, cities as varied as Boise, Idaho, and Zaragoza, Spain, were scheduled to host anime conventions.

> "I also love the fact that someone can love an anime show so much that they want to get it permanently on their body."[23]
>
> —Tattoo artist Tashy

WHAT IS CRUNCHYROLL?

In America, anime can be found in theaters as well as on cable television networks and familiar streaming services such as Netflix and Hulu. But to truly dive deeply into anime, fans would do well to subscribe to a streaming service known as Crunchyroll.

Established in 2006 by students attending the University of California, Berkeley, Crunchyroll is a streaming service dedicated solely to anime. (In 2020, Crunchyroll was acquired by the Sony Corporation, the electronics manufacturer based in Japan.) Subscribers can find a menu of more than thirteen hundred anime feature films and television series. Crunchyroll is reported to have more than 3 million subscribers in more than two hundred countries. In addition to streaming anime content, Crunchyroll members can also access an online gift shop offering anime-related merchandise for sale. According to tech critics Alex Haslam and Timothy J. Forster,

> Most anime fans are familiar with Crunchyroll, which provides on-demand streams of some of the most popular titles in the genre. Many shows are available within a day of their first streams in Japan, so US-based viewers are able to stay up to date on all their favorites. . . . The brand engages with its audience beyond its streaming offerings, with events like conventions and merchandise sales, which brings a unique value to its viewers.

Alex Haslam and Timothy J. Forster, "Crunchyroll Review and Prices," *U.S. News & World Report,* November 10, 2022. www.usnews.com.

Some twenty thousand fans of anime attended such a convention in Fort Worth, Texas, in December 2022. While attending the convention, they had opportunities to attend panel discussions by anime artists, writers, voice actors, and producers who discussed the process of creating anime series and feature films; visit booths where merchants sold anime-themed goods; and participate in cosplay contests. One of the vendors at the Fort Worth convention was Brennan Enos, a former Fort Worth English teacher who now owns a retail store in the city where he sells anime-themed products. According to Enos, he did not pay much attention to the genre until his two young sons started watching anime television series at home. "The sophistication and sometimes the absolute brilliance of the stories is amazing, so that's what opened the door to anime for us,"[24] explained Enos.

Another attendee at the Fort Worth convention, Rebecca Pineda, said she and her family formerly lived in Japan, where she grew into an avid anime fan. When she was eleven years old, her family moved to Texas, where she soon discovered that anime was hard to find both on television and in the local movie theaters. Pineda said few of her new friends in Texas had any idea of what she was talking about when she would attempt to discuss her favorite anime shows with them. But over the years, Pineda said, anime has grown to be a lot more common, and now, at the age of thirty, she remains a dedicated fan of anime and has little trouble finding the latest series on television and films in the local cinemas. She recalled, "I watched slowly, over the past 20 years, this pop culture trend explode. The very same things that people looked sideways at me for, they're wearing it on their shirts and putting it all over their cars. It's exciting for me to see the culture that I have loved for so long be welcomed with open arms and people line up out the doors for it."[25]

Every year, in cities around the world, devoted fans attend anime conventions like this one in Sydney, Australia. Conventions offer fans a place to interact, dress up, and talk about all of their favorite stories and characters with others who share their enthusiasm.

Morgan Berry has attended several anime conventions—not as a fan, but as a panelist. She is an actress who has provided the English-language voices for characters in many anime television series. She admits,

> I never really expect to see that many people interested in my work. Sometimes I'll get off a panel and then I'll go to my autograph table and I look at the line. The people waiting to get my autograph. It's looping around the entire room and I'm like, what? Surely these people are at the wrong table, right? I'm just like, no way, no they're not here for me. Turns out they are and I'm like, well that's insane.[26]

ANIME ON SOCIAL MEDIA

If fans find themselves counting the days until an anime convention arrives in their city, they need not endure those days alone. Anime fans can find plenty of comradeship online, particularly on social media platforms where they trade opinions about their favorite shows, exchange news about the anime world, and speculate on the future direction of their favorite series.

On Facebook, there are hundreds of groups dedicated to anime, some with millions of followers. In fact, many fans of specific series have started Facebook groups devoted exclusively to those series and their characters. For example, the very popular anime series *One Piece,* which follows the adventures of a group of young treasure hunters known as the Straw Hat Pirates, has prompted its fans to dedicate a Facebook group to the show. By early 2023, the *One Piece* Facebook group counted more than 5.5 million followers. In late 2022, when the captain of the Straw Hat Pirates, Monkey D. Luffy, disappeared after a confrontation with the villain Kaidou of the Beasts, some 250 members of the *One Piece* Facebook group weighed in with opinions on whether Luffy would return to the series. (The general consensus was that the *One Piece* producers would eventually bring Luffy back.)

PODCASTS: FOLLOWING ANIME WITHOUT THE ANIMATION

During the past decade, podcasts have become a familiar source of news, trends, and commentary. Virtually anyone can record podcasts and upload them to numerous hosting sites where they can be heard by listeners. Of course, podcasts are voice recordings; no illustrations or images can be transmitted through them.

But that has not stopped fans of anime from tuning in to dozens of podcasts devoted to the art form. Anime podcasters offer news and commentary about developments in the anime world. Among the most popular podcasts are *Otaku Spirit Animecast, Anime Summit, Suuuper Anime Podcast, Anime at the Gates, Kawaii-FI Radio*, and *Anime Addicts Anonymous*. According to Ed and Solo, who are the hosts of *Suuuper Anime Podcast,*

> [Our podcast] is a show that looks to entertain, inspire and inform you about anime. We provide our opinion and thoughts on various anime topics, as well as look at it from a real-world perspective on what we can learn from anime. Whether you're new to anime or a seasoned veteran, we invite you to come listen, share and laugh with us. We hope every episode ignites your otaku [anime fan] spirit.

Suuuper Anime Podcast, "About Us," 2022. www.suuuperanimepodcast.com.

Fan groups are also prolific on other platforms. Fans of *One Piece* can compare notes on Twitter, where a page devoted to the series counts some 2.4 million followers. On Instagram, a *One Piece* page counts more than 1.6 million members. And on TikTok, hundreds of fans have uploaded their videos filmed with *One Piece* themes; a TikTok page devoted to the show has more than 165,000 followers.

One Piece fans can also log onto YouTube, where followers of the series have created channels devoted to discussions about the show, its characters, and its plot lines. One dedicated fan, who goes by the name of Tekking101, has established just such a YouTube channel. By 2023, followers of the Tekking101 channel numbered more than seven hundred thousand subscribers. And typically, after Tekking101 uploads a video to YouTube, subscribers leave hundreds of comments. For example, in early 2023 Tekking101 devoted a forty-minute video to his speculations on the true role played by the *One Piece* character Stussy, an agent of a secret intelligence network known as Cipher Pol. Within a few days of uploading the video, it had been viewed by about a hundred thousand subscribers, with more than seven hundred subscribers leaving their own comments. Many of the comments focused on whether Stussy was actually another *One Piece* character in disguise.

THE OTAKU CULTURE

Social media can help fans stay connected with the world of anime, but social media has its limits: everything fans may see and experience in the anime world is only visible on the screens of their computers, tablets, and phones. To truly immerse themselves in anime culture, fans may find themselves making trips to Japan to visit the country's so-called otaku districts.

Otaku—which literally means "your house"—started out as a derogatory term, coined by Japanese citizens to describe young people whose interests are focused entirely on manga, anime, and video games. In other words, the otaku continue to live in their parents' homes even as they grow into young adults. The term grew out of a 2004 novel, and later live-action film, titled *Densha Otoko*—in English, *Train Man*—which tells the story of a

One of Japan's best-known otaku districts is Tokyo's Akihabara neighborhood (pictured). Here anime enthusiasts can shop for anime-inspired merchandise ranging from clothing to smartphone cases. They can also eat in cafés staffed by servers dressed as anime characters.

nerdy young man who was so focused on anime that he had no interest in dating or developing the talents he would need to find a career. "Isn't there something odd about a 22-year-old man being so utterly clueless?"[27] asks a film critic for the *Japan Times.*

Older citizens of Japan may have shuddered to believe that young people were turning into members of otaku culture, but many young people embraced the lifestyle. Today, many neighborhoods in Tokyo are dedicated to otaku culture. In these neighborhoods, fans can find numerous theaters that screen anime only. The streets are lined with stores that sell manga and anime on DVDs as well as other merchandise, such as anime-inspired clothing, posters, action figures, smartphone cases, and similar items. Arcades, where fans can play anime-related video games, are common as well. Another familiar feature found in the otaku districts are cafés in which the walls are lined with illustrations of anime characters. Waitresses who work in the cafés dress in uniforms resembling outfits worn by characters in anime television series and films.

In Tokyo, the Akihabara neighborhood is one such otaku district. According to Casey Baseel, an American-born correspondent for a Tokyo-based Japanese news network,

> For fans of Japanese pop culture, the streets of Akihabara have a beauty that's on par with verdant bamboo groves, mist-shrouded mountain temples, or any other representative scenery of Japan. It's the biggest gathering place in the world for otaku artform enthusiasts, an entire urban district devoted to anime, video games, and other forms of passionate expression that have captivated people from around the world.[28]

According to the Japan Tourism Agency, about 1 million foreign visitors travel to Japan each year specifically to tour Tokyo's otaku districts. As for anime fans who have not yet found their way to Tokyo, they can always focus on social media, attend conventions, get tattoos of their favorite characters, and participate in cosplay events to show their devotion to the world of anime.

CHAPTER FIVE

THE FUTURE OF ANIME

The transparent celluloid sheets so vital to enabling artists to develop anime's unique style of storytelling were mostly discarded years ago. Now, anime as well as animation produced in other countries is largely accomplished on the computer. Instead of employing artists to meticulously ink and color thousands of individual cels used to animate a television series or feature film, production companies have turned the job over to animators who sit behind computer screens.

Essentially, the animators who work in computer-generated imagery (CGI) create characters on the screens of their computers. These characters are known in the trade as *skeletons*. The animator can manipulate the skeleton into a variety of poses on the screen. The computer then takes over and fills in the movements of the character between poses. In the past, it could very well have taken hundreds of cels to animate a simple movement by a character. Now, it may take a few keystrokes at the computer.

CGI has enabled anime artists to move beyond those familiar cel-animated static poses and wide-eyed facial expressions and offer audiences true action on the screen. As film critic Maya Phillips notes, "A swimmer's arms cut through the water. A basketball player pivots in a tight semicircle around an opponent. . . . These scenes are animated, but they're no less entrancing than live performance. . . . You can see the beauty of athletes in motion [in] sports anime series like *Haikyuu!!*, *Kuroko's Basketball*, *Free!* and *Yuri!!! on Ice*."[29]

ANIME AT THE CROSSROADS

Phillips and other film critics may be excited by the new trend in anime, but many of anime's longtime fans are not sure they want to see all that action on the screen. Instead, they prefer the stories of anime told in the fashion that gave anime its signature look and unique way of telling stories. "There is a reason why CGI is so heavily criticized," says anime critic Rhytham Das. "The fact of the matter is that the use of CGI heavily deviates from what an anime is supposed to be about. . . . For hard-core anime enthusiasts, the CGI use simply hurts their sentiments, and perhaps even rightly so."[30]

Despite those concerns, when it comes to anime, CGI is here to stay. Indeed, CGI is a far faster process. A computer can animate a scene in the fraction of the time it would take perhaps dozens of artists to produce thousands of cels. And given the current output of Japan's animation studios, which typically produce two hundred television series and films each year, the speed in which CGI animation can be produced is vitally important.

Yet many anime studios realize their fans crave the old-style cel animation and have gone back to incorporating cel animation into some of the scenes of their latest releases. For example, the anime series *Space Battleship Yamato 2199* (a reboot of a 1974 fully cel-animated series) features plenty of high-speed CGI action as the pilots of warring spaceships engage in interstellar dogfights. But the studio has incorporated cel animation for many scenes—mostly for close-ups of the pilots' faces during battle scenes. As anime critic David Carl Cutler points out, "The anime excels when it comes to using [CGI] as extensively as it does. All the ships, including the fighter jets, are animated in [CGI]. This means most of the space fights do not

> "The fact of the matter is that the use of CGI heavily deviates from what an anime is supposed to be about."[30]
>
> —Anime critic Rhytham Das

include traditional animation, outside of the pilots. With a few glaring exceptions, the anime pulls this off superbly."[31]

Cutler believes that anime studios have come to realize that although they must rely on CGI to produce their television series and films, the fans demand a style that does not veer greatly from the anime they have grown to love. He says, "Anime is at a crossroads when it comes to animation. Technological advancements have finally made it possible to consistently use [CGI] animation. However, there are trade-offs to picking either [CGI] or traditional hand-drawn or cel animation. Traditional animation is costly and stiff when done poorly, while [CGI] is fluid but looks out of place when executed wrong."[32]

ANIME IN 3-D

As anime studios search for the proper mix of styles that their fans will accept, the technology continues to move forward. One major innovation that is expected to soon become more common in the anime world is three-dimensional (3-D) animation. In 3-D animation, characters are part of imagery that makes it appear they have depth and texture unavailable on two-dimensional surfaces, such as television or movie screens. The 2009 science fiction thriller *Avatar*, made by a US-based studio, is regarded as a groundbreaking accomplishment in 3-D animation. Since its initial release, the film has earned nearly $3 billion in worldwide box office revenue. A sequel, *Avatar: The Way of Water*, was released in late 2022 and quickly earned more than $2 billion in box office revenue.

Given the success of such 3-D animated films, many anime studios have focused on developing their own 3-D features, but they have yet to achieve the commercial success or popularity of the *Avatar* series. For example, in 2021 the Japanese studio Toei Animation announced plans to release a new chapter in its enormously popular *Dragon Ball* franchise of films, for the first time employing 3-D animation. Akira Toriyama, the artist who created the

ANIME TRANSITIONS TO LIVE ACTION

Superman made his debut in comic books in 1938 and has since gone on to be featured in numerous animated features as well as many live-action films and television series. But as Superman transitioned from comic book character to live-action hero, anime studios were hesitant to turn their characters over to live-action filmmakers. Anime creators feared a backlash from fans who were devoted to the animated versions of their favorite stories.

But that trend started to change over the past two decades as such popular anime series as *Attack on Titan*, *Animal World*, *From Me to You,* and *Death Note* made the transition to live-action films. Even the groundbreaking story of *Speed Racer*, which helped introduce American audiences to anime back in the 1960s, was produced as a live-action film. Anime experts predict that live action will become a bigger part of the anime world in the years ahead. Anime critic Kara Joan Hunsdon comments, "Despite this hesitant audience, the film industry never stops trying to find the perfect balance between bringing anime to life and capturing these characters' emotions, actions, and stories. Some of these adaptations are surprising fan favorites and cult classics that create a smoother-than-expected transition from anime to live action."

Kara Joan Hunsdon, "Live-Action Movies Based on Anime That Are Actually Great," Game Rant, December 1, 2022. https://gamerant.com.

original *Dragon Ball* characters, explained that the studio would "be charting through some unexplored territory in terms of the visual aesthetics to give the audience an amazing ride, so I hope everybody will look forward to the new movie."[33]

The 3-D animated film that was released, *Dragon Ball Super: Super Hero*, premiered in 2022. Longtime fans of anime found themselves less than enthusiastic about the film. Although the film did earn about $86 million in box office revenue, critics and fans were far from satisfied with the finished product. "*Super Hero*'s decision to go 3D was always going to be worrisome," wrote anime critic Rory Wilding. "There are some stunning shots . . . but there is still a stiffness that comes across the character designs that don't feel as expressive. No matter how much the 3D camera swings around the super-powered figures, the action lacks the impact that you would expect from this much-loved property."[34]

Moreover, in 2016 the producers of the original *Sailor Moon* series debuted a three-season reboot titled *Sailor Moon Crystal*, which featured 3-D animation. But again, the 3-D series received a lukewarm reception. Anime critic Rebecca Silverman points out that the poorly executed 3-D animated sequences are most apparent when the Sailor Scouts transform from schoolgirls into superheroes:

> Transformations are the backbone of any magical girl anime, the moment when "ordinary girl" becomes "superheroine." In the first two seasons of *Sailor Moon Crystal* these were handled with questionably rigged and lazily textured 3D computer graphics, taking you out of the magic of the moment as you were struck by how awkward the whole thing looked. While season three still has its odd moments during the transformations, usually limbs bending like wet noodles, the grace has been restored to the process.[35]

Anime critic Callum May suggests that 3-D may not yet be the right platform for anime because anime studios have yet to prove

The success of 3-D animated films such as Avatar and its sequel, Avatar: The Way of Water *(shown),* has sparked interest in many anime studios. Early ventures in 3-D anime have had mixed results.

they are very good at it—and it is easy to see why. Although *Avatar: The Way of Water* earned more than $2 billion very soon after its release, the studio spent more than $250 million to produce the film. That amount included a very big budget for making the 3-D animation realistic. Many Japanese anime studios do not have those resources. That is why the 3-D scenes in anime productions often do not measure up to the expectations of fans. According to May,

> 3D animation is difficult, time-consuming, and expensive. In fact, it's often used hesitantly within 2D anime because of this, and is most commonly used when a scene can't feasibly be created using 2D animation. It's also worth pointing out that while fans sometimes will notice moments of exceptional 3D animation, they'll always notice when it looks awkward or out of place. People are generally more forgiving towards 2D anime. When 2D anime has issues, it just doesn't move much or the character may look a bit wonky, but in the case of 3D anime with production errors, it becomes very obvious with stiff movements, odd lighting, or inhuman movements.[36]

ANIME AND VIRTUAL REALITY

Despite the shortcomings of 3-D technology when applied to anime, experts agree that studios will eventually get it right. Therefore, fans can expect to see studios produce more and more anime featuring 3-D imagery.

Even more technological advancements may be a part of anime's future. Several anime studios are known to be exploring holographic technology—creating a 3-D image without the need for the image to be anchored to a screen. In other words, a theater rigged with holographic projection equipment would be able to show a film unfold as though the characters are real—so real, in fact, that audience members could reach out and touch them. (However, because the characters are composed of light beams, an audience member's finger would pass through the image.) "Imagine the experience is so 'real' that it feels as if you're in the

ANIME OFTEN PREDICTS THE FUTURE

Producers of anime are very good at predicting the future, often conceiving of innovations that eventually find their way into the real world. For example, in 2003 the anime series *Fullmetal Alchemist* featured a character, Edward Elric, who loses an arm and a leg but has them replaced with robotic limbs. In 2015, such technology became available to people whose limbs had been amputated due to illnesses or accidents.

Artificial intelligence (AI) is quickly becoming a part of modern life as computer-driven machines—among them, self-driving automobiles—learn to think for themselves. An early concept of AI was introduced back in the 1990s, first in the anime television series *Digimon: Digital Monsters* and then in the 2000 film *Digimon: The Movie*. The television series and film told of children and their lovable (and, occasionally, evil) robot pets that could think for themselves. Anime critic Victor Santiago recalls,

> When I first watched *Digimon*, I knew that *Digimon* was short for "Digital Monster" . . . but it wasn't until I revisited the series that the technological side of *Digimon* became apparent. Despite being very science fiction, *Digimon* always felt like a fantasy. As I got older and started to understand concepts like artificial intelligence and virtual reality, I also began to see the real-world possibility behind *Digimon*.

Victor Santiago, "We Came of Age with *Digimon*," SYFY, July 31, 2020. www.syfy.com.

same room as the anime characters," says anime critic Theo J. Ellis. "And with the way technology is growing, it won't surprise me when something like this is possible."[37]

Ellis also expects virtual reality (VR) to become a big part of the anime experience. VR headsets have been a popular form of entertainment for several years. Users put on the headsets, often inserting their phones, which are equipped with apps for the headsets. (Some VR headsets are "stand-alone" devices, meaning the content is already loaded in them.) While using the VR headsets, users can play e-sports games—competing in slalom ski races, battling terrorists, or facing an opponent in the martial arts—while never leaving their living rooms.

Anime-style games and characters have been a part of the video game universe for many years. Available for such platforms as the Microsoft X-Box and Sony PlayStation, video game titles include *Final Fantasy XV*, *Attack on Titan,* and *Sword Reverie*. Now, anime-style action has also transitioned into VR headsets and is expected to become a significant player in the video gaming experience. For example, anime critic Adam Braunstein enthusiastically endorses the VR game version of the television series *Attack on Titan:*

> *Attack on Titan* is one of the best and most popular anime of all time. It's extremely unique among most anime because its crazy concept involves the invasion of gigantic . . . humans that terrorize the inhabitants of a walled-in city. That unique concept didn't exactly scream VR adaptation, but sure enough, just that has happened. . . . It's absolutely thrilling to soar through the air at these horrific beings with your dual swords at the ready to deliver a finishing blow. This one can get pretty dizzying after a while, so don't play for too long if you've had issues with motion sickness in VR in the past.[38]

> **"It's absolutely thrilling to soar through the air at these horrific beings with your dual swords at the ready to deliver a finishing blow."[38]**
>
> —Anime critic Adam Braunstein

Anime fans are fickle. On the one hand, they are willing to dive deeply into the latest technology, such as VR, but they do not want to see that technology change the anime they have grown to love. As anime moves into the future, the Japanese studios producing the television series, films, and video games know they must tread a narrow path that ensures the traditional style of the art form they created decades ago does not create a dramatic new look that will alienate their long-devoted fans.

SOURCE NOTES

INTRODUCTION: ANIME AT THE OLYMPICS

1. Quoted in Danica Davidson, "Uzbekistan Rhythmic Gymnastics Team Performed as Sailor Moon," *Otaku USA,* August 10, 2021. https://otakuusamagazine.com.
2. Katie Gill, "How *Sailor Moon* Revolutionized the Magical Girl Genre," Tor.com, July 12, 2022. www.tor.com.
3. Quoted in Jamie Lang, "'It's Time That People Really Start Taking This Seriously': Anime Is Booming at the US Box Office," Cartoon Brew, November 4, 2022. www.cartoonbrew.com.

CHAPTER ONE: THE EVOLUTION OF ANIME

4. Quoted in Jonathan Clements, *Anime: A History.* New York: Bloomsbury, 2022, p. 124.
5. Clements, *Anime*, p. 48.
6. Susan Napier, "Not Always Happily Ever After," in *Fairy Tale Films Beyond Disney: International Perspectives,* edited by Jack Zipes, Pauline Greenhill, and Kendra Magnus-Johnston. New York: Routledge, 2016. Kindle.
7. Quoted in Patrick Brzeski, "How Japanese Anime Became the World's Most Bankable Genre," *Hollywood Reporter,* May 16, 2022. www.hollywoodreporter.com.

CHAPTER TWO: THE STORIES TOLD THROUGH ANIME

8. Melissa See, "*Yuri!!! on Ice*," in *Anime Impact: The Movies and Shows That Changed the World of Japanese Animation,* edited by Chris Stuckmann. Coral Gables, FL: Mango, 2018, pp. 438–39.
9. Patrick Drazen, *Anime Explosion: The What? Why? and Wow! of Japanese Animation*. Berkeley, CA: Stone Bridge, 2014, p. 14.
10. Isaiah Colbert, "This New Romance Anime Is a Breath of Fresh Air After Last Year's Harem Blitz," Kotaku, January 4, 2023. https://kotaku.com.

11. Chris Stuckmann, *"Your Name,"* in *Anime Impact: The Movies and Shows That Changed the World of Japanese Animation,* edited by Chris Stuckmann. Coral Gables, FL: Mango, 2018, p. 436.
12. Via Erhard, "12 Most Twisted Dark Anime Series," Game Rant, November 9, 2022. https://gamerant.com.
13. Alexander Case, "Anime Review: *Tokyo Mew Mew New,"* *Breaking It All Down* (blog), September 25, 2022. https://countzeroor.com.

CHAPTER THREE: THE UNIQUE STYLE OF ANIME ART

14. Susan Napier, "Manga and Anime: Entertainment, Big Business and Art in Japan," in *Routledge Handbook of Japanese Culture and Society,* edited by Victoria Lyon Bestor and Theodore C. Bestor. New York: Routledge, 2011, p. 232.
15. Christopher Hart, *Anime Mania: How to Draw Characters for Japanese Animation.* New York: Watson-Guptil, 2002, p. 7.
16. Hart, *Anime Mania,* p. 7.
17. Christopher Hart, *Manga for the Beginner: Everything You Need to Start Drawing Right Away.* New York: Watson-Guptill, 2008, p. 32.
18. Hart, *Manga for the Beginner*, p. 126.
19. Hart, *Manga for the Beginner,* p. 130.
20. Jordan C. Stewart, *"Teen Titans*'s Anime Influence—Character Design," *Cinema Anime* (blog), February 11, 2019. https://eng345anime.wordpress.com.

CHAPTER FOUR: THE CULTURE OF ANIME

21. Quoted in Olivia Singh, "Ariana Grande Got a New Tattoo That Honors One of Her Favorite Movies," *Insider,* August 29, 2018. www.insider.com.
22. Quoted in Kaytlin Waddington, "10 Times Megan Thee Stallion Showcased Her Love for Anime," Comic Book Resources, September 26, 2022. www.cbr.com.
23. Quoted in *Rooster,* When It Comes to Anime or Manga Tattoos in Colorado, Tashy Is Blowing People Away," January 12, 2022. https://therooster.com.
24. Quoted in Marcheta Fornoff, "Anime Frontier Returns to Fort Worth Convention Center," KERA News, December 2, 2022. www.keranews.org.
25. Quoted in Fornoff, "Anime Frontier Returns to Fort Worth Convention Center."

26. Quoted in Chandra Traxler, "How Anime Is Taking Over the Western Audience," Medium, March 5, 2021. https://ctraxler.medium.com.
27. Quoted in Matt Alt, "The United States of Japan," *New Yorker,* May 4, 2018. www.newyorker.com.
28. Casey Baseel, "This One Photo Shows How Tough Times Are in Tokyo's Akihabara These Days," SoraNews24, July 22, 2021. https://soranews24.com.

CHAPTER FIVE: THE FUTURE OF ANIME

29. Maya Phillips, "What Can a Body Do? Anime Pushes at Its Limits," *New York Times,* September 2, 2020. www.nytimes.com.
30. Rhytham Das, "Why Fans Are Justified to Hate the CGI in Chainsaw Man Anime Leaks," Spiel Times, October 4, 2022. www.spieltimes.com.
31. David Carl Cutler, "10 Best Anime That Mixed Traditional & 3-DCG Animation," Comic Book Resources, August 11, 2022. www.cbr.com.
32. Cutler, "10 Best Anime That Mixed Traditional & 3-DCG Animation."
33. Quoted in Anthony Nash, "Akira Toriyama Admits *Dragon Ball Super: Super Hero* Title Is 'a Bit Repetitive,'" ComingSoon, January 21, 2022. www.comingsoon.net.
34. Rory Wilding, "'Dragon Ball Super: Super Hero' Is Super Disappointing," AIPT Comics, August 18, 2022. https://aiptcomics.com.
35. Rebecca Silverman, "The Rebirth of *Sailor Moon Crystal*," Anime News Network, July 22, 2016. www.animenewsnetwork.com.
36. Callum May, "2D and 3D: Creating the Anime of the Future," Crunchyroll, October 29, 2017. www.crunchyroll.com.
37. Theo J. Ellis, "The Future of Anime: Big Changes We're Likely to See Because of Technology," Anime Motivation. https://animemotivation.com.
38. Adam Braunstein, "Best Anime VR Games," Ready VR One. https://readyvrone.com.

BOOKS

Toshio Ban, *The Osamu Tezuka Story: A Life in Manga and Anime*. Albany, CA: Stone Bridge, 2022.

Jonathan Clements, *Anime: A History*. New York: Bloomsbury, 2022.

Gianni Simone, *Otaku Japan: The Fascinating World of Japanese Manga, Anime, Gaming, Cosplay, Toys, Idols and More!* Rutland, VT: Tuttle, 2022.

Bradley Steffens, *The Art and Artists of Anime*. San Diego: ReferencePoint, 2022.

Nao Yazawa, *Drawing and Painting Anime and Manga Faces: Step-by-Step Techniques for Creating Authentic Characters and Expressions*. Beverly, MA: Quarry, 2021.

INTERNET SOURCES

Patrick Brzeski, "How Japanese Anime Became the World's Most Bankable Genre," *Hollywood Reporter*, May 16, 2022. www.hollywoodreporter.com.

Katie Gill, "How *Sailor Moon* Revolutionized the Magical Girl Genre," Tor.com, July 12, 2022. www.tor.com.

Jamie Lang, "'It's Time That People Really Start Taking This Seriously': Anime Is Booming at the US Box Office," Cartoon Brew, November 4, 2022. www.cartoonbrew.com.

Maya Phillips, "What Can a Body Do? Anime Pushes at Its Limits," *New York Times*, September 2, 2020. www.nytimes.com.

Kaytlin Waddington, "10 Times Megan Thee Stallion Showcased Her Love for Anime," Comic Book Resources, September 26, 2022. www.cbr.com.

WEBSITES

AnimeCons

https://animecons.com

The organization that plans anime conventions provides a schedule of upcoming events on its website. Visitors can also find videos of cosplay contests featured at many past conventions, news of developments in the anime industry, and a link to the AnimeCons YouTube channel, which features interviews with voice actors, producers, and other creative people in the anime industry.

Anime News Network

www.animenewsnetwork.com

Fans of anime can find news about the latest releases of television series and films, reviews, and commentary on trends in anime. Among the tabs available to visitors are "Live-Action," which updates fans on the latest anime films to be adapted into live-action films, and "Encyclopedia," in which fans can find profiles of anime voice actors and other key figures in anime production.

Christopher Hart Books

https://christopherhartbooks.com

The American anime and manga teacher Christopher Hart maintains this website to share his expertise with students on how to draw the components of anime and manga. Among the tabs available on the site is "New Videos," which provides links to Hart's YouTube channel in which he offers instruction on how to draw the characters featured in anime and manga.

Comic Book Resources

www.cbr.com

The website covers the worldwide animation and comic book community with a tab dedicated solely to anime. By accessing the tab, visitors can find reviews of the latest film and television anime releases. There are also separate tabs within the anime section of the site that enable visitors to read reviews and updates on the anime features *One Piece* and *Dragon Ball.*

Crunchyroll

www.crunchyroll.com

This website, maintained by the popular anime streaming service, provides subscribers with lists of anime films and television series available for viewing, but visitors can find an abundance of free content, including interviews with anime creators, e-book versions of manga titles that can be read online, and previews of films that are slated to appear in theaters.

Suuuper Anime Podcast

www.suuuperanimepodcast.com

This website, maintained by *Suuuper Anime Podcast* hosts Ed and Solo, features archived editions of their past podcasts exploring news and commentary on anime features. The "Blog" tab provides abbreviated reviews by the hosts of new anime releases, and the "Guests" tab provides shortcuts to the podcasts that feature interviews with noted figures in the anime world.

INDEX

PICTURE CREDITS

Cover: Adnin Mourin/Shutterstock

 6: Reuters/Alamy Stock Photo

 9: NBC/Photofest

10: Lion's Gate/Photofest

15: Everett Collection Historical/Alamy Stock Photo

19: Olga Besnard/Shutterstock

21: Associated Press

24: BFA/Alamy Stock Photo

30: Jemastock/Shutterstock

33: Chatchai Somwat/Shutterstock

35: TCD/Prod.DB/Alamy Stock Photo

38: United Archives GmbH/Alamy Stock Photo

41: mjmediabox/Alamy Stock Photo

44: usia83/Shutterstock

48: DC Studio/Shutterstock

51: Pictorial Press Ltd/Alamy Sock Photo

53: charnsitr/Shutterstock